Finding the Right Words

Finding the Right Words

PERFECT PHRASES TO PERSONALIZE YOUR GREETING CARDS

J. BEVERLY DANIEL

POCKET BOOKS

New York • London • Toronto • Sydney

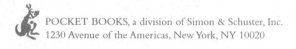 POCKET BOOKS, a division of Simon & Schuster, Inc.
1230 Avenue of the Americas, New York, NY 10020

ISBN: 0-7434-7719-7

First Pocket Books hardcover edition October 2003

20 19 18 17 16 15 14

Manufactured in the United States of America

For information regarding special discounts for bulk purchases, please contact
Simon & Schuster Special Sales at 1-800-456-6798 or business@simonandschuster.com

To

John

Tracey, George, Eric

And especially to my granddaughter,

Molly

Acknowledgments

I am grateful to my dad and mom, Frank Hoffman and the late Mildred Hoffman, for their unwavering support and faith in me to never give up my dreams. They gave me the courage to follow through and complete my book.

To my brothers, John, Greg, and Joe, thank you for your support. Greg, you have always been my sounding board, and special thanks to Joe, without whose help this book would never have been completed.

To my editor, Micki Nuding, many thanks for the enthusiasm and interest she has shown for this project. I have really enjoyed working with Micki and greatly appreciate her expertise.

Many thanks to my wonderful agent, Mary Tahan, as well as Stedman Mays and Jena Anderson of Clausen, Mays & Tahan Literary Agency. Without their vision, faith, and encouragement none of this would have been possible. When at times things became overwhelming, Mary's encouragement put me at ease and back on track.

Contents

Introduction xi

Introduction

Throughout the fifteen years that I was in the card and gift shop business, my customers often asked me to help them find the right words to say what they felt, whether they were wishes for a happy birthday, congratulations on the birth of a child, or condolences on the death of a loved one.

No matter how beautiful a greeting card and its verse, nothing means more than the handwritten note added inside the card. It is the most important and meaningful part of the card.

But from time to time, we all have difficulty coming up with the appropriate phrase. How many times have we struggled to find the right words, especially for a sympathy or get-well card? Sometimes our mind draws a blank.

Finding the Right Words is the answer to this problem: it's a quick and easy-to-use reference guide designed to jump-start you in the writing process by providing lists of phrases, words, and sentiments for most occasions.

You will also find useful information for card mailing. "Helpful Hints" gives you tips on how to be more organized and efficient in your card giving, so you never have to send a belated card again. There are also monthly lists for birthdays and anniversaries, state abbreviations, and pages for your holiday card lists.

There are so many uses for *Finding the Right Words*! Besides helping you with preprinted cards and blank notes, some of the phrases also make perfect "toasts" for special occasions such as weddings, retirements, etc. This book itself makes an excellent gift to include in a gift basket, or a great stocking stuffer at Christmastime.

And don't feel locked into using the phrases as they are: change them around to suit the occasion or the person to whom you are writing; feel free to be creative with them! And if you don't find what you need in one section, check the other sections, as some phrases are interchangeable. Or combine phrases to fit the occasion.

Greeting cards are a permanent and meaningful method of communication. Emails and phone calls are wonderful, but they're gone as soon as you hit the SEND button, or hang up the receiver. After an occasion has passed, we often hang onto the memories, the photos, and the greeting cards. This book is my gift to you, to help you create personal messages on cards that loved ones will hold onto as keepsakes forever.

Occasions

Birthday

May all your wishes come true

Many happy returns

How is it that birthdays don't show on you? You've gotta tell me
your secret . . . and don't give me that business about a painting
in the attic.

Have a wonderful birthday

It's all right to light the candles on your birthday cake now; I have
alerted the fire department.

Have fun on your birthday

Every birthday holds the promise of a new beginning. Hope this is
your best year yet!

Have a sensational birthday

I hope this birthday is the happiest yet

Happiness on your birthday and always

Happy ___ birthday. Are you counting in dog years?!

Your birthday is a day that should go down in history (unless you
    have finally succeeded in destroying all the copies of your birth
    certificate in the public records office)

The only way to look younger is to be born later

"Formula for Youth"—count your blessings, not your wrinkles

Youth happens, but age is earned

Birthdays are an opportunity to reconnect with those we care
    about. Even though we're far apart, I'm with you in spirit on
    your special day.

Some people make the world brighter just by being in it

I love sending you a birthday card, because you've always been and
    always will be older than me!

Being born is a miracle—and I think you're absolutely miraculous!
    Have a wonderful birthday.

When things start to sag, and things start to drag, when you stand
    on your head, they don't look so bad!

Birthday, shmirthday . . . who's counting?

50? Let's not go there.

Now we're so old, we have to take a nap before we blow out our
    birthday candles!

God's blessing always

Hope your birthday is as happy as you've made me

Have a happy birthday and a great year

I hope all your birthday wishes come true

May your birthday be filled with wonderful surprises

Remembering you on your birthday and always

May your birthday be bright and beautiful

May God bless you on your birthday and always

May your birthday be as special as you are

A birthday hello to keep in touch

I remember when we used to shop for each other's birthday gifts in the petite department. What on earth are we doing in the "women's" sizes now?

May a special person have a special birthday

Much love on your birthday and always

Sending warm wishes for your birthday always

May this year bring you closer to all your dreams and wishes

Wishing you all the happiness that you so deserve

Friends are never far apart on their birthdays

Hope your birthday is all you wished it would be

May your birthday be simply the best ever
Wishing you a beautiful birthday filled with love and laughter
This birthday greeting comes across the miles with a big hug
Happy birthday to someone who has always been there for me
Happy birthday to a forever friend

"A woman's always younger than a man of equal years."
—*Elizabeth Barrett Browning*

Wedding Anniversary

Love makes a house a home

Congratulations! You've tangoed for ___ years and you're still both in step!

You both share a very special love

Wishing you every happiness as you celebrate the love you share

Wishing you a beautiful day and many more happy years

Youth may fade, but a lasting love grows more radiantly beautiful with each day

May love always live in the home you share

We wish you all the happiness the coming years can hold

We're wishing everything wonderful to a wonderful couple

Hope your special day is made up of sharing warm and happy memories

Time has distilled the essence of your love

Let space travelers discover new galaxies in the universe; I am content to marvel at the preciousness of your love

May your love bring happiness to all your days

May this special day be filled with joy, love, and laughter

Wishing you a lifetime of love

May all your days be filled with lasting love

Love is when two hearts beat as one, as your two hearts have for the past ___ years, with many more to come . . .

Let us celebrate the faithfulness of your enduring union—through good times and bad—in a world of ever-shifting change

The love you share makes this day special

May every year you share find you more in love with each other

May your future be as happy and bright as your anniversary

May today be as memorable as the day you were married

May your anniversary be filled with treasured memories

Wishing you a special anniversary and many more years of happiness

All the best to you both on your anniversary and in the wonderful years to come

Only 50 years? See, and they said it wouldn't last!

May all your dreams come true on your anniversary and always

May your love continue to grow with each passing year

May the happiness of this day continue for the rest of the year

May joy and happiness be yours today, tomorrow, and always

How could you put up with each other for so many years? It must be love!

Wishing you sunny days and moonlit nights

May the celebration of your love continue forever

Wishing you much love on this special day

Congratulations and best wishes to you both for the future

May the love you share today bring you happiness forever

Wishing you a lifetime of love, laughter, happiness

May you share a wonderful day and a wonderful life

Wishing you both continued love and happiness

"He is happiest, be he king or peasant, who finds peace in his home."

—*Johann von Goethe*

"The supreme happiness in life is the conviction that we are loved."
—*Victor Hugo*

Anniversary to Spouse

I may not say the words very often, but my heart is full of love for you

When I married you, I married for "better or worse." When does the worse start?

When I think of all the special moments we've shared through the years, I fall in love with you all over again

I love you even more today than the day we were married

I am so lovingly grateful for everything you do for me, even if I seldom show it

Our years together have been so wonderful. Isn't it time for separate vacations?

Of all the people in the world, I'm so glad we found each other

Just to keep you on your toes . . . I like to introduce you as "my *first* husband"!

As we celebrate our anniversary, I just wanted to let you know how much your love has meant to me

Through all the happy times and sad times, our love has been the glue that holds us together

Our life together has brought me such happiness and contentment

I can't believe we've been married for ___ years. I still feel like a newlywed.

The secret of our happy marriage is two words . . . "Yes, dear!"

You make life so interesting and exciting. I don't know what I would do without you.

I hope I have made you as happy as you have made me

You have been my spouse, my lover, my best friend and confidant

There are so many things I have been thankful for through the years, but you top the list

Nothing makes me happier than waking up to see your smiling face

This is only the beginning of the rest of our life together

You make it so easy to love you with all my heart

What makes our marriage so happy are the many happy memories we share and treasure

There are so many ways you make me happy, but drinking out of
the carton is not one of them!

"Being deeply loved by someone gives you strength; loving
someone deeply gives you courage."

—*Lao-tzu*

"Life's greatest happiness is to be convinced we are loved."

—*Victor Hugo*

"The important thing was to love rather than to be loved."

—*W. Somerset Maugham*

". . . For thy sweet love remembered such wealth brings that then I
scorn to change my state with kings."

—*William Shakespeare*

"Let me confess that we two must be twain, although our undivid-
ed loves are one."

—*William Shakespeare*

Wedding and Engagement

Wishing you happiness every day

You both deserve the very best that life can bring you

May all the dreams you are dreaming soon turn into dreams
    come true

He chased you with so much enthusiasm that you finally caught him!

Congratulations on finding each other

May the joy you share grow deeper day by day

Today is meant to be treasured

The honeymoon is so short-lived, enjoy it while you can!

You both deserve a lifetime of beautiful tomorrows

All the best—to the best

May God bless your union for all time

May you treasure today forever in your memories

May all the love you have come to know continue to grow

Enjoy your wedding . . . it's the best part of a marriage!

Open your heart to someone you love, and the world opens up to you

Sharing your life with someone you love, makes the journey sweet

The best is yet to come

Sharing in your happiness and wishing you all the best

Blessings for your new life as husband and wife

May the joy you share today grow deeper through the years

Wishing you happiness and joy in this new life you share

You are off to a beautiful beginning

Have a wonderful life together

Wishing you companionship, contentment, and love

Wishing you a wedding day full of all the love your hearts can hold

May your love endure forever, or until your first argument!

Wishing a special couple many happy memories

The happiest marriage starts with the comfort of just being together

To the perfect couple on their special day

May your marriage be filled with health, wealth, and a sense of
humor

May this be the beginning of a lifetime of love and happiness

May the circles of your rings remind you of your never-ending love

Cherish your love and each other

The glue that holds two people together is love and a great sense of humor

Hoping your special day and your future are full of happiness and joy

May your memories of this day live on forever

Wishing you a day filled with love and happiness

May God's blessing be yours forever

May many wonderful moments make up your special day

May your life together be all you dreamed it would be

Wishing you a lifetime of happiness

Wishing all your tomorrows are as happy as today

May your love continue to grow with each passing year

"The Constitution only gives people the right to pursue happiness. You have to catch it yourself."

—*Ben Franklin*

"He conquers who endures."

—*Persius*

"Friendship often ends in love; but love in friendship—never."
—*Charles Caleb Colton*

18 *J. Beverly Daniel*

New Baby

Babies are God's miracles

A baby is a bundle from Heaven

Congratulations on your new little someone to love

A new baby gives us the gift of innocence

Everything else comes with a book of instructions; why doesn't a baby?

Congratulations on your new little bundle of blessings

A baby's smile makes each day worthwhile

It's hard to tell who is luckier, you or your new baby

Grandchildren are a mother's way of getting even with her children!

Even the angels smile when a baby laughs

The waiting is finally over and you have a bundle of joy to love

We're so happy about the arrival of your new addition

Congratulations on your new tax deduction!

To the darling little newcomer

How happy you must be with a new little daughter/son to love

I don't want to tell you how to raise your baby, but . . .

Having a newborn teaches us how to love again—unconditionally

How your home has been blessed with a new baby!

May your new little daughter/son bring you joy and happiness

Parenthood is one of the greatest joys in life

Having a baby is like finding a treasure in your own backyard

Babies are such fun, until it's time to change their diapers!

With the first touch of your baby's hand, you know there is a God

A baby is held briefly in your arms but forever in your heart

God bless you and your new baby on this special day

It's great to be a grandparent. All the fun and none of the problems!

There is nothing more precious than a new baby to love

May your new baby bring you joy and happiness forever

A baby is one of life's treasures

With your new baby, your life is now complete

Love to the new baby and best wishes to all

Congratulations on the new love in your life

Wishing you all the happiness parenthood brings

Sending you warm wishes to welcome your new little angel

May the wonder of a new baby bring much happiness to your home

May your new baby make life more exciting with each passing day
I know you will find your new baby is a blessing from above
May your new baby fill your life with happiness, joy, and lots of
    laughter

" 'Tis a happy thing to be the father unto many sons."
                               —*William Shakespeare*

"A child of our grandmother Eve, a female; or, for thy more sweet
    understanding, a woman."
                                 —*William Shakespeare*

"A mother's pride, a father's joy."
                                 —*Sir Walter Scott*

Thank You

Your thoughtfulness really put sunshine in my day

Thank you for your thoughtful hospitality

Thank you for being so nice

How beautiful a day can be when kindness touches it

Because of you, everything is so much nicer

Thank you for making a stranger feel like one of the family

Your thoughtfulness will long be remembered

Thank you from the bottom of my heart

I'm more thankful than mere words can ever tell

Your kindness comes as a welcome touch of warmth and caring

So thoughtful of you to think of us

Thank you for making me feel so comfortable

Thank you for making your guests feel right at home

Your kindness meant so much

Thank you for the great gift. What was it again?

Many thanks for the wonderful dinner. Being with you was as
    delicious as the food!

This comes with sincere appreciation

You always do the nicest things in just the nicest way

The world's a better place because of people like you

Your thoughtfulness meant more than words can ever say

It's so difficult to say thank you. So I won't!

Every time I look at the gift you gave me [or "the flowers you
    sent," etc.], I think fondly of you. You're a sweetheart.

You always go out of your way to be thoughtful

Words say so little when someone's done so much

Thank you for being you

Thank you for the little things you so often do

Thank you for your strength and support

Your act of kindness has not gone unnoticed

Your kindness is a treasured keepsake

Your kindness and generosity have always made you a special person
    to me

May all the thoughtful things you do for others be returned to you
    tenfold

I just can't seem to thank you enough

Thank you for being there for me

A simple thank-you is so inadequate for all you have done

Your thoughtfulness was appreciated more than words can ever say

Thank you for your kindness and compassion

Special thanks for making our day special

Thank you for being there for me and being my friend

Thank you for going out of your way to make our stay so pleasant

With sincere gratitude for all you have done

Thank you for the comfort and understanding you have given me

Your support has meant so much to me

Get Well

Hope you'll continue to feel better every day

Hope you're up and about soon

Hope you're feeling better

Wishing you a speedy recovery

We're *sick* without you—get well soon!

Just a cheery note to wish you well

Hope your hospital stay is a short one

Hope you'll soon be well

Beyond every cloud, there is a rainbow

May God bless you and keep you in His loving care

Hoping this finds you well on the way to a speedy recovery

It's a hard way to get a mini-vacation from work!

Smiles are the best medicine

Wishing you the very best of health

Hope you'll be feeling frisky again in no time

Did you figure out a way to warm up the bedpan yet?

By the time this reaches you, I hope you'll be well on the road to a speedy recovery

Hope you'll be in the best of health again soon

Hoping each new day will find you feeling better

Be sure to ask the doctor where that stick has been before you say, "Ahhh"!

May your days ahead be filled with sunshine and roses as your health returns

Thinking of you and hoping you're feeling better soon

Wishing you warm and sunny wishes for a speedy recovery

Thinking of you and hoping you're feeling better

I hope your illness will soon be only a memory

May God be watching over you during your time of illness

So sorry to hear you are not feeling well, and hope you'll soon be as good as new

Glad to hear it's only a cold and you'll be up and around in two to three months!

You are in my prayers for a speedy recovery

Hoping you're feeling stronger with each passing day

With love and special wishes that you'll soon be feeling better

Hope your hospital stay is short, unless the doctors/nurses are cute!

Hope this message cheers you and that you're feeling much better

Thinking about you often and wishing you a speedy return to good health

Sorry you're not feeling well and hoping you'll soon be feeling better

Sending you peaceful thoughts and warm wishes

Just a note to let you know how much I care

My thoughts are with you with love and caring

"The best way to cheer yourself up is to try to cheer somebody else up."

—*Mark Twain*

Friendship

It's wonderful sharing with a good friend like you

Happiness is having a friend like you

Friends are forever

I'm a much better person for having known you

Thank you for being my friend

Nothing can separate friends

Your friendship means so much to me

Our friendship doesn't dare break up. We know too much about
each other!

A friend is someone you can lean on

You're a priceless gem, and I treasure you

Fair weather, foul weather—I can depend on you and that means a lot

True friends show themselves in adversity as well as triumph. You've
been so good to me, let me return the favor sometime.

Remember the time we . . . oops, we don't want the kids to see
     that!

Friends make life more beautiful

It is a rare friendship that feels forever new

It's so nice sharing special moments with a friend like you

Friends don't always say what we want to hear, but thanks for being
     honest with me

Thanks for being a good enough friend to tell me the truth; I
     needed to know

Life is made up of a patchwork of friends

We've had our share of arguments, but thank heaven one of us isn't
     stubborn!

To someone I can always talk to

Thoughts of you always bring me a smile

Friends are never apart

A friend is forever

Our friendship is golden

For a special friend

Friendship keeps hearts in touch

"Though we travel the world to find the beautiful, we must carry it with us or we find it not."

—*Ralph Waldo Emerson*

"The only way to have a friend is to be one."

—*Ralph Waldo Emerson*

"But if the while I think on thee, dear friend, all losses are restored and sorrows end."

—*William Shakespeare*

Congratulations

Hoping the best things in life will always be yours

Congratulations and best wishes always

Heard you were a winner, but I knew that already

An effort a day keeps failure away

With warmest congratulations

Winning is sweet, isn't it? And you've got plenty more victories ahead.

So happy to hear your good news

You came through with flying colors

This is a day to remember

Congratulations on passing your driver's test! A whole new world
will now open up to you.

You held onto your dreams, and your wishes came true

Congratulations on breaking free and accomplishing your goal

You made the team. Way to go!

We are so proud of your accomplishment

You have worked so hard and gained so much
You passed your driver's test. Don't forget to let me know when
    you'll be on the road!
So happy to see you have broadened your horizons
Congratulations on your much-deserved promotion
Congratulations on succeeding after many obstacles
This is only the beginning of a journey to bigger and better things
It was an outstanding accomplishment
Your success is an inspiration to everyone
You met the challenge head-on and won
Congratulations on a job well done
We are all so proud of your achievement
No one deserves the award more than you

"The rung of a ladder was never meant to rest you, but only to
    hold a man's foot long enough to enable him to put the other
    somewhat higher."

—*Thomas Henry Huxley*

Graduation

You've taken a big step on the yellow brick road. Now you're on
   your way to Oz!

To graduate with high honors is a major achievement

I so admire the determination you displayed in achieving your goals

Congratulations on your promotion to the ___ grade. I'm so proud
   of you!

I can't believe you finally made it. Must be a mistake!

You finally graduated, and without my help. How did you do it?

We're so proud of the perseverance you showed in reaching for the
   stars and getting them

You have worked so hard and deserve many congratulations on
   your achievement

Graduate? Any genius can do that!

Your brilliant future has now begun

Graduation is quite a milestone in your pursuit of a great career

Congratulations, graduate. Success is in your future.
All your hard work has finally paid off

" 'He means well' is useless unless he does well."

—*Plautus*

"Go confidently in the direction of your dreams. Live the life you
have imagined."

—*Henry David Thoreau*

Bon Voyage

Embrace your new lands with open arms

Thank heaven you're leaving . . . otherwise, I'd never know how
much I miss you!

Your dreams have come true. You're finally taking the trip of a
lifetime.

Have a great cruise. Relax, eat, dance under the stars, and have fun!

Have a great time on your trip, and don't forget my surprise!

You'll have a great time, and all I'll get is a lousy postcard!

Leave your cares and problems behind and have a great trip

Leave the snow behind and enjoy the balmy breezes and tropical
nights

Please think of us slaving away as you're sipping your Mai Tai!

May your trip be all you dreamed it would be

I will be lonesome without you, but have a great time

I will be thinking about you as you're winging your way to _____

Retirement

Don't look at retirement as the end of something; it's the beginning
   of newfound freedom

Hope this day will be the start of the best of everything for you

You're retiring? You mean you've been working?!

May retirement be the beginning of your happiest years

May your days be full of fun and laughter during your retirement

Now that you've given to the world, it's time to give to you

Wherever you go and whatever you do, may sunshine follow you

May the coming years bring you much happiness

Now you can finally fluff-off and get paid for it!

Have yourself a wonderful day and a great future

Wishing you life's best

May every happiness be yours today and forever

Hoping all your dreams become reality

Wishing you the best of everything today, tomorrow, and always

Now that you're retired, you can tell your wife how she's been
  doing her housework all wrong!
May this day and every day be perfect for you
From today on, may all your wishes and dreams come true
May your days be filled with love, peace, health, and happiness
Wishing you all life's best, today and always
Retirement means you can finally be annoying all the time!
May each year bring you added happiness
It's finally time for swaying palms, umbrella drinks, and a suntan!
This is the time when you can finally shut off the alarm and go
  back to sleep!
All the hobbies you have been putting off are yours to explore now
It's time to go fishing and catch a real record breaker
Think of retirement as a permanent vacation, and only work when
  you're in the mood

Sympathy

Please accept our deepest sympathy and heartfelt thoughts

May time accomplish what no words can do

Words are so inadequate at a time like this

May God be with you at this time

There is so little one can say, but my heart goes out to you

My heart is reaching out to you in sympathy and prayer

May the comfort of friends and family be your strength now and in the days ahead

May God hold you in His arms and heal the sorrow that you feel

May God hold you in the palm of His hand and comfort you with His everlasting love

Our sympathy and warmest thoughts are with you now

Expressing sympathy is always difficult, but all we can say is how sorry we are

We're with you in our thoughts today

Our thoughts are with you in this time of sorrow

May memories be a source of comfort at this time

May it help to know that friends are sharing the sorrow in your
heart

Wishing you God's peace

May time be a source of healing for you

May you be comforted by our sincere thoughts and prayers

Please remember that God is always there to comfort you

Please remember that if you need us, we're only a phone call away

Hope these words convey our heartfelt sympathy at your time of
loss

Sometimes things are easier to bear when you know friends care

May time and love bring you peace

With sincere and heartfelt sympathy in your time of sorrow

Sharing in your sorrow and offering deepest sympathy

May the love of family and friends bring you peace and comfort

May you find consolation in the thought that God is with you
always

Caring thoughts are with you

Hoping my deepest sympathy brings you comfort in some small way

May you find consolation in knowing that others care

Please remember that your loss is shared by those who care and understand

May God's love give you strength during your time of sorrow

Sharing your sorrow in the loss of your loved one

Hoping these words of sympathy will comfort you in your time of sorrow

You're in my thoughts and in my prayers

People pass on, but their memory lives on in our hearts

"His cares are now all ended."

—*William Shakespeare*

"We are in God's hand."

—*William Shakespeare*

"Everyone can master a grief but he that has it."

—*William Shakespeare*

Sympathy II
Condolence Thank-You

A sincere thank-you for your thoughts and prayers

Please accept my heartfelt thanks for your kind words of comfort

I greatly appreciate everything you have done for me and my family

Thank you for the many thoughtful things you have done for us

I just wanted to let you know how grateful I am for all the help
  you gave me during this difficult time

Having someone to lean on during this sorrowful time was greatly
  appreciated

You don't know what your expression of sympathy has meant to me/us

Your compassion has been a source of comfort and warmth during
  this difficult time. You're a blessing.

Knowing how much friends care during this difficult time has made
it easier to bear

With all the difficult decisions to be made at this time, you have
been a great help to me

Your words of comfort were gratefully appreciated

New Home

A home is a house filled with love

Every happiness in your new home

May peace and love abide with you in your new home

After interviewing hundreds of housekeepers and consulting with
Martha Stewart, I've found the perfect gift for your new home—
hope you like the spatula!

Congratulations on your new home

May your new home be filled with love and laughter

God bless your happy home

Happy nesting!

May your new home bring you peace, comfort, and joy

May the only problems you have in your new home be little ones

May you live happily ever after in your new home

Don't forget to put *snowblower* and *lawnmower* on your
housewarming gift list!

Wishing you everything good in your new home

Wishing you happy days and friendly neighbors

We're so happy that you found your dream home

May you find peace and happiness in your new home

May the joy you shared in your apartment double in your new home

With sincere wishes for all your dreams to come true in your new home

There is something so special about owning your own home

It's your house, and you can finally do what you want with it!

With all good wishes to you and yours in your new home

We were so delighted to hear about your new home

May many happy new memories begin in your new home

May your future in your new home be filled with much joy and laughter

A home is just a house if there's no laughter in it

Thinking of You

Thinking of you and wishing you a happy day

We do not remember days; we remember moments

For someone too special to ever forget

When this you see, think of me

Every time I sit down for a cup of coffee/tea, I can't help but think
of you

When I think of you, so many happy memories come flooding
back

I miss our many heartfelt conversations

You know so many of my secrets, we had better keep in touch!

Every time I see a beautiful sunset, I think of you

I miss you more and more every day

Remember the time . . . oops, I guess I had better not get into that!

I remember all the fun we had during every change of season

Because you touched my life so deeply, I think of you often

Whenever I see the first snowfall, I always think of you
We share so many memories, and I love to stay in touch
Thinking of you with gratitude and respect
Just to let you know you are in my thoughts and prayers daily
Thinking of you with love and affection
So much has gone on in our lives, and I'm so glad we were there
    for each other

"Some cause happiness wherever they go, others whenever
    they go."

———*Oscar Wilde*

"The most wasted day of all is that during which we have not
    laughed."

———*Sébastien–Roch Nicolas Chamfort*

"The human race has one really effective weapon, and that is
    laughter."

———*Mark Twain*

Apology

It was my fault and I'm sorry

I was so inconsiderate and I apologize

Sometimes a puff of smoke clears the air. I'm sorry!

Forgive me, I was wrong

Please accept my sincerest apology

I'm so sorry for what I said. Now what was it again?

You were right, I'm an idiot

Please forgive me for being so late. It was inexcusable.

My actions proved how thoughtless I can be

One of us should apologize!

I messed up. I'll try to do better.

I'm to blame and I would like to make amends

I think we're both feeling a little bruised by our last conversation, so let's
    talk again soon. I want you in my life. I know we can work things
    out. Our relationship adds up to much more than our last fight.

I hope you can forgive me for what I have done
Me wrong. You right. Sorry.
My sensitivity was on vacation that day and I'm so sorry
Please accept my deepest regrets for hurting your feelings

"For all sad words of tongue or pen, the saddest are these: 'It might
    have been!' "

—*John Greenleaf Whittier*

"To err is human; to forgive, divine."

—*Alexander Pope*

Divorce

Divorce is not the end of the world. It can be a beautiful beginning.

I heard you lost 180 ugly pounds. Congratulations on your divorce!

It took a lot of courage, but you were right to leave him

Sorry to hear about your divorce. Just remember that family and
friends are here for you.

No more frogs!

Free. Free. Free at last . . . Thank God you're free at last!

Sometimes the only solution to an unhappy marriage is divorce

You put your heart and soul into your marriage, and I'm so sorry it
didn't work out

Congratulations on your divorce. Now you can finally start living.

Your newfound freedom will make you feel as though you were
living in a bad dream

Live, love, laugh, and be happy

Now you have a chance to find your real Prince Charming
Your heart might be broken today, but I guarantee it will mend
   sooner than you think

Pets

FOR A NEW PET:

I hear the pitter-patter of tiny paws at your house—congratulations
   on your new kitty/puppy

A new puppy/kitten really makes a happy home complete

Wishing you much fun and laughter with the arrival of your new pet

I hear you have some new arrivals! Congratulations on your new
   puppies/kittens/etc.

There is nothing like a songbird to brighten up your day

GET WELL:

Hope your puppy's nose will soon be cool and his/her tail wagging
   again

Hope your cat will be purring and his/her tail flicking again soon

Sorry to hear about your pet's accident. Hope he/she will soon be on the road to recovery.

Hope all goes well with your pet's surgery and he/she has a speedy recovery

So glad to hear your pet's surgery went well and he's/she's bouncing around

DEATH OF A PET:

The passing of a pet is like losing a member of the family

May memories of happy times console us when our pet is no longer with us

May the happy memories of your pet ease the pain of his/her loss

A pet is always an important part of the family and your loss was felt deeply by all

BIRTHDAY GREETINGS:

It's your dog's birthday; may he/she receive many dog bones!
It's your cat's birthday; may he/she receive many toys!

GENERAL:

A pet is a lot of work, but he/she gives such unconditional love
There is nothing like being greeted at the door by a wagging tail
Cats are so much fun, but they have their own special way of
    making you feel guilty
A pet can sense when you don't feel well, and bring a smile to
    your face

Relatives

_____ are forever, and I'm so glad you're mine

To a _____ who is a forever friend

_____ are for caring and sharing

_____ are for hugging

_____, you're loved a lot

With a _____, there is a warmth that is seldom spoken

Happiness is having a _____ for a best friend

A _____ is someone you would like to be like

My _____ always—now, too, a friend

For a _____ who means so much

To a very special _____

A _____ is a lifelong friend

To the world's greatest _____

To _____ with love

_____ are for loving

A _____ is a very special blessing

There is no dearer friend than a _____

_____, you are always in my thoughts

Happiness is having a _____ like you

Love is another word for _____

A _____ is a forever friend

Happiness is being married to you

To the love of my life

Step-Relatives

Happiness is having a stepmother for a best friend

For a stepfather who means so much

Ever since Snow White, stepmothers have gotten a bad rap. But
   you've always made me feel like the apple of your eye.

A stepsister is a lifelong friend

As a stepbrother, you are a true friend

You shine extra bright for the choice you made to love me

I consider you more of a mother than a stepmother

I am so fortunate to have you for a stepfather

I'm so glad you *stepped* into my life

If I had had my choice of a stepsister, I would have picked you

My stepbrother is a buddy forever

I know you are my stepmother, but I always think of you as Mom

Thank you for choosing to love me

The bond between us is more than stepfather to stepson

We couldn't be closer if we were blood sisters

You are more like a brother to me than a stepbrother

I think of us as more than a stepmother and stepdaughter

You make it so easy to love a stepson

Our family is complete with you as my stepdaughter

I could not picture having anyone else as a stepson

I am so grateful that you are my stepmom

I am so blessed to have a stepdad as great as you

My stepfather always has a special place in my heart

Being a stepmother is no easy job, but you make it seem so easy

General

To someone who is always close to my heart
My heart will always save a special place for you
A friend knows everything about you and likes you anyway
Sending this for no special reason other than to say Hi
It takes someone special to be a friend
Sending heartfelt wishes for a perfect day
I was opening a can of beans and it made me think of you.
    Hmmmm!
Hope your special day is as special as you are
Our friendship means more to me with each passing day
Wishing you an abundance of happiness on this very special day
Why is it that when I'm having a bad day, I think of you?!
You're in my thoughts always
May your every wish come true today, tomorrow, and always
May God's gift of love be yours forever

Warm and friendly wishes forever

Thinking of you with affection

Sending hugs and kisses on your special day

Just thinking of you puts a smile on my face. Weird, isn't it?

May you always be as happy as you are today

Wishing much happiness to a very special couple

May your tomorrows be just as special as today

Sharing your joy for today and wishing you happiness always

May you enjoy each day more than the day before

Thanks to the greatest grandparents for continuing to spoil me,
   even though I'm all grown up

Grandpa, thank you for giving me the courage to learn to ride my
   bike

I learned all my cooking skills from you. Thanks, Grandma.

If I could have chosen my grandparents, I would have picked you

Mother's Day

Our conversations over a cup of coffee always mean so much to me

Mom, you've taught me so much, and these are the values I will
keep for a lifetime

We may not always see eye to eye, but I always value your opinion

Thanks for loving me, no matter what

Though you threatened to put me up for adoption many times, I'm
grateful you didn't!

Mom, now that I am a mother, I finally understand with appreciation what you went through

Whatever was broken, I didn't do it. My brother did!

With love and appreciation for all the things you've done for me

Thank you for always being there for me

Wishing you all the happiness you so richly deserve

You are not only my mother, but also my best friend

It is so difficult to put into words all the love and appreciation I feel

I never gave you any gray hairs! Did I?

A mother is for caring and sharing, and loving

Without you, Mom, the world would be a dreary place

A mother may not always be right, but she is never wrong

Thank you for your unconditional love

We have never been closer and I am so thankful

I love you, Mom. Now, do I still have to clean my room?

A mother is a very special blessing

Happiness is having a mother like you

May all your wishes come true on Mother's Day and always

Through your love and care, you have made a house a home

Many happy memories come flooding back on Mother's Day

A mother is someone you can lean on

There is nothing more comforting than a mother's hug

You can always count on Mom to tell you the truth

"The mother's heart is the child's schoolroom."

—*Henry Ward Beecher*

"Motherhood: All love begins and ends there."

—*Robert Browning*

"The heart of a mother is a deep abyss at the bottom of which you will always find forgiveness."

—*Honoré de Balzac*

"Men are what their mothers made them."

—*Ralph Waldo Emerson*

"All that I am, or hope to be, I owe to my angel mother."

—*Abraham Lincoln*

"The hand that rocks the cradle is the hand that rules the world."

—*W. R. Wallace*

Father's Day

One of my happiest memories is of our many walks and talks

Thank you for always being there for me and understanding

Thank you for always protecting me from the storm

I just wanted to let you know how much I appreciated all the times
  you stopped what you were doing just to listen to me

Dad, you have always been so special to me

Thank you for your unconditional love

Thanks for always knowing when to hold me tight and when to let
  me go

The values you gave me I will treasure forever

Your guidance and advice is what made me what I am today

Every gray hair you have you owe to me!

Many happy memories come flooding back on Father's Day

With love and appreciation for all the things you've done for me

You have taught me so much, from riding a bike to driving a car.
   Thanks, Dad.

Thank you for always listening and understanding

Your love and wisdom have made me what I am today

I am so proud that you are my father

Dad, you have been my rock!

This is your special day, Dad, so relax and enjoy it

Me, late for curfew? Never!

Wishing you all the happiness you so richly deserve

I have always valued your opinion and treasured your love

By the way, I wasn't the one who decorated the walls with your
   shaving cream. My sister did it!

Whether it's been a broken heart or a leaky faucet, you have always
   been there for me

I never get tired of hearing your stories about the "old days"

Thank you for your sense of humor. It got me out of trouble
   many times!

Just to let you know how much I love you and appreciate you

Dad, you have always been my hero and best friend

Your kindness and caring has always been an inspiration to me

If I could have had my choice of dads, I would have picked you
You were the only person who could make me laugh when I
was sad

"It is a wise father that knows his own child."
—*William Shakespeare*

"Men of few words are the best men."
—*William Shakespeare*

"Wit and wisdom are born with a man."
—*John Selden*

"One father is more than a hundred schoolmasters."
—*George Herbert*

Valentine's Day

My heart belongs to you on Valentine's Day and always

For my soul mate and best friend

You complete me

Will you be mine on Valentine's Day and forever?

You are sweeter than candy and lovelier than a rose

You have stolen my heart forever

Roses are red, violets are blue, Valentines used to suck, but now
there's you!

Looking forward to sharing my Valentine's Day with my sweetheart

Twinkle, twinkle, little star, I wanna get you drunk in a really dark bar!

Love and kisses now and always

Sending you a big hug on Valentine's Day

Hoping this card warms your heart with happy memories

With you, it's no more black and white. It's Technicolor and
Surround Sound!

This is the perfect day for candlelight and romance

This Valentine card comes with much affection

A thousand kisses . . .

Please "bee" mine because you are my "honey"

Happy Valentine's Day to the most special person in the world

The thought of you makes me blush

Our love is very special to me

Thank you for putting sunshine in my life today and forever

Without you . . . what's the point?

Valentine's Day is the perfect time to say how much you mean to me

My romantic dreams pale with the reality of you

Tonight is made for moonlight and romance

No card can convey how deep my feelings are for you

Valentine's Day is a day for remembering

I just wanted to let you know how happy you make me on
    Valentine's Day and every day

"At the touch of love everyone becomes a poet."

—*Plato*

"A very small degree of hope is sufficient to cause the birth of love."

—*Stendhal*

"Men always want to be a woman's first love—women like to be a man's last romance."

—*Oscar Wilde*

"There is no remedy for love but to love more."

—*Henry David Thoreau*

"From fairest creatures we desire increase, that thereby beauty's rose might never die . . ."

—*William Shakespeare*

". . . If I could write the beauty of your eyes and in fresh numbers number all your graces . . ."

—*William Shakespeare*

"Shall I compare thee to a summer's day? Thou art more lovely and
   more temperate."

—*William Shakespeare*

". . . Gentle thou art, and therefore to be won . . ."

—*William Shakespeare*

Easter

May the Easter season bring you peace and happiness always

Hoping your Easter is happy and blessed

May your Easter basket be filled to the brim with goodies

Wishing you joy and peace at Easter and always

Hoping the Easter season finds you blessed with health and
happiness

All good wishes for a very happy Easter

May the wonderful blessings of Easter be with you always

Hoping your heart is filled with joy this Easter season

May this Easter season be filled with happiness for you and those
you love

Warmest Easter wishes from our home to yours

I heard the Easter bunny is bringing something extra special

Hoping your Easter is a most joyous holiday

May you and your family have a blessed Easter

May you rejoice in this happiest of seasons
Sending sincere wishes for all the happiness of this Easter season
Thinking of you on this Easter holiday
Remembering many happy memories at Easter and always
May your Easter be filled with family and joy
Sending you a happy Easter along with hugs and kisses
May you rejoice in God's blessing on this happy Easter

Passover

Best wishes for a warm and happy Passover

May you know peace and happiness during the Passover holiday

Sending Passover greetings and thinking of you often

May this important Jewish festival find you all happy and healthy

May you have a joyous Passover

Wishing you and your family peace and happiness during your
Passover celebration

Hoping this holiday season finds you with many happy memories

With sincere wishes for a very happy Passover

May the peace of this season be with you always

Wishing a special Mom and Dad a special and happy Passover

Grandma and Grandpa, missing you and remembering many happy
memories of past Passover celebrations

May your heart be filled with joy on this happy Passover season

May the spirit of Passover bring you contentment

Warmest wishes for a happy Passover from our home to yours

May love, hope, and happiness be yours at Passover and always

May your Passover celebration be filled with joy and delight for you
and those you love

Wishing someone who is close to my heart a very happy Passover

Sending warm and friendly wishes for Passover and always

Friends are never really that far apart at Passover

Hanukkah

Wishing a bright and happy Hanukkah to you and your loved ones

Hoping this Hanukkah season finds you healthy and happy

Sending you Happy Hanukkah wishes

May the lighting of the Hanukkah candles bring you joy and peace

This is a time to bring your family near and hold traditions dear

Thinking of you and your family during this glorious eight-day
   celebration

Sending you the gift of love during this happy Hanukkah season

Wishing you the peace of the season during this time of joy

With each candle lit, may your heart be warmed and your soul
   satisfied

Sending blessed sentiments along with a happy Hanukkah

So many happy memories of you come flooding back during the
   Hanukkah celebration, Grandma and Grandpa

Tradition warms the heart, satisfies the soul, and brings families
together to remember what it's all about

Mom and Dad, you have always made this such a happy season for us

Sending warm Hanukkah wishes to you and yours

Because of you, the traditions of Hanukkah have always meant so
much to me

Wishing you peace and prosperity during Hanukkah and always

Sending you Hanukkah greetings and thinking of you often

This happy season means even more when you can share it with
friends

Hoping your Hanukkah celebration will be a joyful occasion for
you and your family

May your Hanukkah season be filled with love, laughter, and peace

Sending you all the peace and happiness the season brings

May this festive season find you and your loved ones with many
happy memories

Kwanzaa

Hoping your Kwanzaa celebration will be a joyful occasion for you
  and your family

Sending you the warmest of Kwanzaa wishes

May the spirit of Kwanzaa be in your heart always

Wishing you unity and love on this joyous occasion

May the lighting of the candles illuminate the pride you feel

Celebrate the Seven Principles of Kwanzaa with great joy

Thinking of you during Kwanzaa and always

Thinking of the Kwanzaa feast brings back many happy memories

The gathering of family and friends means even more during
  Kwanzaa

Kwanzaa gives more meaning to life

May the Kwanzaa holiday find you and your family well and happy

May your Kwanzaa celebration bring you closer to your African
  history and heritage

Though I cannot be with you during this wonderful Kwanzaa celebration, I will be there in mind and spirit

Best wishes for peace, health, and happiness on this happy holiday

Warmest wishes from our home to yours during this holiday season and always

In the true spirit of the Kwanzaa celebration, wishing you peace and joy

May the peace and unity you share at this time last forever

Have faith and believe in yourself, and happiness will follow

This is the season for pride and commitment for you and those you love

May this time of celebration and reflection be a treasured memory always

Christmas

May your heart be filled with every joy this lovely season brings

Wishing special joy for you at Christmastime and all year through

May the wonderful blessing of Christmas remain yours throughout
the year

Warm wishes for a wonderful Christmas and happy New Year

Warmest greetings of the season and best wishes for the coming
year

Best wishes for peace, health, and happiness

Hope you have the merriest Christmas ever

May the spirit of Christmas bring you peace and joy

All good wishes for a happy holiday season and a prosperous New
Year

Wishing you all things bright and beautiful at Christmas and all year

Warmest holiday wishes from our home to yours

In the true spirit of the season, wishing you peace and joy

May your Christmas be blessed with peace and happiness

May love, hope, and happiness be yours at Christmas and always

Hope your holidays are happy days!

May this season be filled with joy and delight for you and those
you love

Wishing you the warmest, merriest Christmas and happiest
New Year

Have a wonderful Christmas and the best of everything in the
New Year

Wishing a bright and happy holiday to you and those you love

Deck the halls with houghs of bolly . . . oops . . . too much eggnog
again. Oh well, Merry Christmas!

Helpful Hints
to Simplify Card Sending

Are you sometimes late getting out your greeting cards? Or do you sometimes even forget to send them altogether? Do you always promise yourself that this year things will be different, that you'll definitely get that birthday card out to your sister *before* her birthday—but somehow, once again, you don't?

I know how it is; we're all busy, and we don't seem to have the time to shop for cards, much less write them and get them in the mail on time.

But it doesn't have to be this way.

Here are some helpful hints to help you organize and simplify the task of sending greeting cards.

   • Turn to the Calendar section of this book and fill
   in the names, birthdays, and other dates you wish to

remember for all your family and friends, including anniversaries, Valentine's Day, etc. (If you don't wish to use the Calendar section of this book, then be sure to add these dates to your address book.)

• Include the *year* of the births and weddings; that will tell you which birthday or anniversary is being celebrated.

• In your purse, keep a copy of the filled-in monthly Calendar pages, or your address book with birth dates and wedding dates penciled in, or a list of the names, birth dates, and anniversary dates in your wallet.

• Purchase all the cards you will need for each month of the year at least a month in advance. Since you will be carrying the dates with you at all times, you can easily refer to your list any time you're in a bookstore, card shop, or other store that sells greeting cards.

• Once you've purchased the cards, write the mailing date in the stamp corner of the envelope. After you've stamped the envelope, the date will be covered and out of sight.

• Put Post-it notes with the name of the recipient on each of the cards.

• Put a shiny sticker on your calendar on the days when cards are due to be mailed.

• Be prepared to send an unexpected card by keeping a box of blank notes, some stamps, and *Finding the Right Words* at home, at your workplace, or in your car.

• Try to include a little gift such as a bookmark, small pin, tiny book, etc. If this isn't possible, include a cartoon or article or picture you think the recipient would enjoy.

• Always date the inside of the card, so in later years the recipient will know when it was sent.

Monthly Calendar for Names, Birthdays, and Anniversaries

(Be certain to include the year!)

JANUARY

Name

Birthday   Anniversary

Name

Birthday   Anniversary

Name

Birthday   Anniversary

Name

Birthday   Anniversary

Name

Birthday   Anniversary

JANUARY

Name

Birthday   Anniversary

Name

Birthday   Anniversary

Name

Birthday   Anniversary

Name

Birthday   Anniversary

Name

Birthday   Anniversary

Name

Birthday   Anniversary

Name

Birthday   Anniversary

Name

Birthday   Anniversary

FEBRUARY

Name

Birthday   Anniversary

Name

Birthday   Anniversary

Name

Birthday   Anniversary

Name

Birthday   Anniversary

Name

Birthday   Anniversary

Name

Birthday   Anniversary

Name

Birthday   Anniversary

Name

Birthday   Anniversary

FEBRUARY

Name

Birthday   Anniversary

Name

Birthday   Anniversary

Name

Birthday   Anniversary

Name

Birthday   Anniversary

Name

Birthday   Anniversary

Name

Birthday   Anniversary

Name

Birthday   Anniversary

Name

Birthday   Anniversary

Name

Birthday   Anniversary

Name

Birthday   Anniversary

Name

Birthday   Anniversary

Name

Birthday   Anniversary

Name

Birthday   Anniversary

Name

Birthday   Anniversary

Name

Birthday   Anniversary

Name

Birthday   Anniversary

MARCH

Name

Birthday .... Anniversary ....

Name

Birthday .... Anniversary ....

Name

Birthday .... Anniversary ....

Name

Birthday .... Anniversary ....

Name

Birthday .... Anniversary ....

Name

Birthday .... Anniversary ....

Name

Birthday .... Anniversary ....

Name

Birthday .... Anniversary ....

APRIL

Name

Birthday   Anniversary

Name

Birthday   Anniversary

Name

Birthday   Anniversary

Name

Birthday   Anniversary

Name

Birthday   Anniversary

Name

Birthday   Anniversary

Name

Birthday   Anniversary

Name

Birthday   Anniversary

APRIL

Name

Birthday   Anniversary

Name

Birthday   Anniversary

Name

Birthday   Anniversary

Name

Birthday   Anniversary

Name

Birthday   Anniversary

Name

Birthday   Anniversary

Name

Birthday   Anniversary

Name

Birthday   Anniversary

MAY

Name

Birthday   Anniversary

Name

Birthday   Anniversary

Name

Birthday   Anniversary

Name

Birthday   Anniversary

Name

Birthday   Anniversary

Name

Birthday   Anniversary

Name

Birthday   Anniversary

Name

Birthday   Anniversary

MAY

Name

Birthday .... Anniversary

Name

Birthday .... Anniversary

Name

Birthday .... Anniversary

Name

Birthday .... Anniversary

Name

Birthday .... Anniversary

Name

Birthday .... Anniversary

Name

Birthday .... Anniversary

Name

Birthday .... Anniversary

JUNE

Name

Birthday   Anniversary

Name

Birthday   Anniversary

Name

Birthday   Anniversary

Name

Birthday   Anniversary

Name

Birthday   Anniversary

Name

Birthday   Anniversary

Name

Birthday   Anniversary

Name

Birthday   Anniversary

JUNE

Name

Birthday   Anniversary

Name

Birthday   Anniversary

Name

Birthday   Anniversary

Name

Birthday   Anniversary

Name

Birthday   Anniversary

Name

Birthday   Anniversary

Name

Birthday   Anniversary

Name

Birthday   Anniversary

JULY

Name

Birthday   Anniversary

Name

Birthday   Anniversary

Name

Birthday   Anniversary

Name

Birthday   Anniversary

Name

Birthday   Anniversary

Name

Birthday   Anniversary

Name

Birthday   Anniversary

Name

Birthday   Anniversary

JULY

Name

Birthday   Anniversary

Name

Birthday   Anniversary

Name

Birthday   Anniversary

Name

Birthday   Anniversary

Name

Birthday   Anniversary

Name

Birthday   Anniversary

Name

Birthday   Anniversary

Name

Birthday   Anniversary

AUGUST

Name

Birthday   Anniversary

Name

Birthday   Anniversary

Name

Birthday   Anniversary

Name

Birthday   Anniversary

Name

Birthday   Anniversary

Name

Birthday   Anniversary

Name

Birthday   Anniversary

Name

Birthday   Anniversary

AUGUST

Name

Birthday   Anniversary

Name

Birthday   Anniversary

Name

Birthday   Anniversary

Name

Birthday   Anniversary

Name

Birthday   Anniversary

Name

Birthday   Anniversary

Name

Birthday   Anniversary

Name

Birthday   Anniversary

SEPTEMBER

Name

Birthday   Anniversary

Name

Birthday   Anniversary

Name

Birthday   Anniversary

Name

Birthday   Anniversary

Name

Birthday   Anniversary

Name

Birthday   Anniversary

Name

Birthday   Anniversary

Name

Birthday   Anniversary

SEPTEMBER

Name

Birthday   Anniversary

Name

Birthday   Anniversary

Name

Birthday   Anniversary

Name

Birthday   Anniversary

Name

Birthday   Anniversary

Name

Birthday   Anniversary

Name

Birthday   Anniversary

Name

Birthday   Anniversary

Name

Birthday   Anniversary

Name

Birthday   Anniversary

Name

Birthday   Anniversary

Name

Birthday   Anniversary

Name

Birthday   Anniversary

Name

Birthday   Anniversary

Name

Birthday   Anniversary

Name

Birthday   Anniversary

OCTOBER

Name

Birthday   Anniversary

Name

Birthday   Anniversary

Name

Birthday   Anniversary

Name

Birthday   Anniversary

Name

Birthday   Anniversary

Name

Birthday   Anniversary

Name

Birthday   Anniversary

Name

Birthday   Anniversary

NOVEMBER

Name

Birthday   Anniversary

Name

Birthday   Anniversary

Name

Birthday   Anniversary

Name

Birthday   Anniversary

Name

Birthday   Anniversary

Name

Birthday   Anniversary

Name

Birthday   Anniversary

Name

Birthday   Anniversary

NOVEMBER

Name

Birthday   Anniversary

Name

Birthday   Anniversary

Name

Birthday   Anniversary

Name

Birthday   Anniversary

Name

Birthday   Anniversary

Name

Birthday   Anniversary

Name

Birthday   Anniversary

Name

Birthday   Anniversary

DECEMBER

Name

Birthday   Anniversary

Name

Birthday   Anniversary

Name

Birthday   Anniversary

Name

Birthday   Anniversary

Name

Birthday   Anniversary

Name

Birthday   Anniversary

Name

Birthday   Anniversary

Name

Birthday   Anniversary

DECEMBER

Name

Birthday   Anniversary

Name

Birthday   Anniversary

Name

Birthday   Anniversary

Name

Birthday   Anniversary

Name

Birthday   Anniversary

Name

Birthday   Anniversary

Name

Birthday   Anniversary

Name

Birthday   Anniversary

State Abbreviations

How many times have you sat down to address an envelope and found you had no idea what to write for the state abbreviation? Is AK Alaska or Arkansas? Is MO Missouri or Montana? The following list solves that problem:

Alabama–AL

Alaska–AK

Arizona–AZ

Arkansas–AR

California–CA

Colorado–CO

Connecticut–CT

Delaware–DE

Florida–FL

Georgia–GA

Hawaii–HI

Idaho–ID

Illinois–IL

Indiana–IN

Iowa–IA

Kansas–KS

Kentucky–KY

Louisiana–LA

Maine–ME

Maryland–MD

Massachusetts–MA

Michigan–MI

Minnesota–MN

Mississippi–MS

Missouri–MO

Montana–MT

Nebraska–NE

Nevada–NV

New Hampshire–NH

New Jersey–NJ

New Mexico–NM

New York–NY

North Carolina–NC

North Dakota–ND

Ohio–OH

Oklahoma–OK

Oregon–OR

Pennsylvania–PA

Rhode Island–RI

South Carolina–SC

South Dakota–SD

Tennessee–TN

Texas–TX

Utah–UT

Vermont–VT

Virginia–VA

Washington–WA

West Virginia–WV

Wisconsin–WI

Wyoming–WY

Holiday Card Recipients

CHRISTMAS

....

....

....

....

....

....

....

CHRISTMAS

....

....

....

....

....

....

....

....

....

....

....

....

....

....

....

....

CHRISTMAS

....

....

....

....

....

....

....

....

HANUKKAH

HANUKKAH

....

....

....

....

....

....

....

....

HANUKKAH

HANUKKAH

....

....

....

....

....

....

....

....

KWANZAA

KWANZAA

....

....

....

....

....

....

....

....

KWANZAA

KWANZAA